LESSER KNOWN

and Curious Water

By the same authors:

THE WATER OF LIFE : SPRINGS AND WELLS OF MAINLAND BRITAIN

By Ian Thompson:

THE LOST SAINTS OF BRITAIN

CONSTANCE SHACKLOCK : A BIOGRAPHY

EARLY HERMIT SITES AND WELL CHAPELS

SAINTS CHURCHES HOLY WELLS

TURN UP THE STONE

BREAKFAST UNDER THE BEAN TREE

By Frances Thompson:

THE ORTHODOX COMPANION & SURVIVAL GUIDE

LENTEN COOKERY BOOK

LESSER KNOWN WELLS
and Curious Water Sources

by

IAN AND FRANCES THOMPSON

BLUESTONE BOOKS

2015

Published by BLUESTONE BOOKS

259 Ashby Road, Scunthorpe. DN16 2AB

Printed by BookPrinting UK

© Ian and Frances Thompson 2015

All rights reserved. No part of this publication may be reproduced, stored in a retrieval system, or transmitted, in any form or by any means, electronic, mechanical, photocopying, recording or otherwise, without the prior permission, in writing, of the publisher.

FRONT COVER ILLUSTRATION

Old Man's Mouth, East Ayton, North Yorks

ISBN 978-0-9931509-0-6

ACKNOWLEDGEMENTS

Our grateful thanks are due, in the first place, to the following:

The Administrator of the Anglican Shrine of Our Lady of Walsingham (the Right Reverend Lindsay Urwin, OGS) for permission to reproduce the official photograph of the Shrine Well on page 46;

Mr Julian Lowe of Nottingham, to whom we are indebted for the photograph of the Malvhina Spout (page 39);

Mr Geoff Brown, Chairman, Troutbeck Village Association, who drew our attention to the Dawson family and their association with local wells (pages 70-71);

Gillian M. Huggins, Co-ordinator, Bathampton Local History Research Group, who undertook a painstaking search for information about the Dog's Head Fountain (page 19). Little is known about this curious feature, and we are grateful to her for unearthing several indirect references to its earlier existence.

We also wish to thank all those nameless individuals – local librarians, pub landlords and their customers, property owners, casual passers-by – who supplied us with information about local wells, directed us when we were lost, or gave us permission to view wells on private land (and in one case entertained us with coffee and cakes!) It is the help and interest of other people that makes well research such a richly satisfying activity.

Ian and Frances Thompson
Scunthorpe January 2015

Temple well, Ujjain, India

CONTENTS

INTRODUCTION	9
GAZETTEER:	
Alkborough, North Lincolnshire: *The Kell Well*	16
Bathampton, Somerset: *The Dog's Head Spout*	18
Bodmin, Cornwall: *St Guron's Well & others*	19
Caistor, Lincolnshire: *The Syfer Spring*	22
Calverton, Buckinghamshire: *Gorrick's Well*	24
Cattistock, Dorset: *Churchyard Well*	25
Conisbrough, South Yorkshire: *The Holy Well*	26
East Ayton, North Yorkshire: *Old Man's Mouth*	28
Fountains Abbey: North Yorkshire: *Robin Hood's Well*	29
Frome, Somerset: *The Holy Well*	32
Giggleswick, North Yorkshire: *Bank Well*	34
Great Asby, Westmorland (Cumbria): *St Helen's Well*	35
Great Hatfield, East Yorkshire: *St Helen's Well*	37
Great Malvern, Worcestershire: *The Malvhina Spout*	40
Hackness, North Yorkshire: *Bridge Springs*	41
Holywell, Huntingdonshire: *The Holy Well*	42
Hope Bagot, Shropshire: *St John the Baptist's Well*	43
Kingsteignton, Devon: *Honey Well*	45
Linby, Nottinghamshire: *Well and Two Crosses*	46
Little Walsingham, Norfolk: *Shrine Well*	47
Llanrhyaedr, Denbighshire: *Ffynnon Dyfnog*	49
Llantwit Major, Glamorgan: *Monastery Spring*	51
Malham, North Yorkshire: *Malham Cove*	52

Matlock Bath, Derbyshire: *Petrifying Springs*	55
Middlesmoor, North Yorkshire: *The Blacksmith's Well*	56
Newtondale, North Yorkshire: *Newtondale Spring*	58
North Cave, East Yorkshire: *St Helen's Well*	60
Sawley, North Yorkshire: *Wine Wife Well*	62
Silverdale, Lancashire: *Woodwell*	63
Southam, Warwickshire: *The Holy Well*	65
Stevington, Bedfordshire: *The Holy Well*	67
Stoke St Milborough, Shropshire: *St Milburga's Well*	68
Stoney Middleton, Derbyshire: *St Martin's Well*	69
Totnes, Devon: *The Leechwell*	70
Troutbeck, Westmorland (Cumbria): *Village Wells*	71
Upwey, Dorset: *The Wishing Well*	73
Watnall, Nottinghamshire: *The Holy Well*	75
Wells, Somerset: *Cathedral Wells*	76
Whitchurch, Buckinghamshire: *Whittle Hole*	79
Widecombe-in-the-Moor, Devon: *The Saxon Well*	80
Wolsingham, Co. Durham: *The Holy Well*	82
Wormhill, Derbyshire: *Brindley Memorial Well*	85
Yeovil, Somerset: *Ninesprings*	86
Appendix A: The Fourteen Best Wells	89
Appendix B: Christianity and Pagan Wells	91

INTRODUCTION

With one or two exceptions holy wells are not spectacular objects, but they do have the capacity to appeal to something deep and mysterious within us. Nothing, you may say, is as commonplace as water, but holy wells are a link with other, earlier worlds: with standing stones, sacred trees and ancient rituals; or, conversely, with ancient churches, hermit sites, and Christian saints. Perhaps too there is the fact that water flows, sparkling and pure, out of the murky depths of the earth. And then water from a holy well can have strange properties. It may turn objects to stone, change colour in a quite extraordinary way, ebb and flow like the sea, or make strange noises. Strangest of all is the thought that, in one or two cases, the water which we see flowing so placidly out of the earth last saw the light of day when it fell as rain in British hills before men learnt to write, or even to smelt iron.

Nowadays when people think of a well they usually have in mind a deep vertical shaft, perhaps with a bucket and winding gear, as in the popular image of a wishing well. Yet with very rare exceptions holy wells are not wells in that sense. Typically they are springs which issue from a rock face or an earth bank and are provided with some sort of tank or basin into which the water falls and from which it can be drawn off for drinking purposes. Some of them – especially mineral springs – have larger tanks or 'baths' in which people used to immerse themselves. Sometimes they are enclosed within an attractive well-house, or are adorned with some other kind of superstructure. This all adds to the visual interest of the well.

What *is* a holy well? Before the introduction of piped water, wells of the kind we have just been describing were to be found everywhere in Britain, and the vast majority of them were not 'holy' – they were just village wells: the only supply of water available to most households. But many villages had one well (and sometimes more than one) about which legends were told, or which was thought to have health-giving properties, or which was regarded with superstitious awe. In most cases it didn't stop people drawing water from the well, but it did invest it with a certain importance – or with a certain inconvenience if it attracted too many visitors or encouraged strange customs, like the hanging of rags on nearby trees. These were what we now call holy wells, and although most of them no longer exist, the wells which do survive tend to be of that kind.

HOLY WELLS – CLASSIFICATION

It is not always easy to classify a well since it may have passed through various 'incarnations', being first of all (say) a Christian well of some kind, later becoming a spa well or (as often happened after the Reformation) attracting to itself residual pagan customs. However the following classification covers most of the wells mentioned in the gazetteer and gives the reader some idea of how holy wells evolved.

1. Pre-Christian and non-Christian pagan wells. Many of these survived into recent times as leftovers, witnessing to ancient beliefs or village superstitions, and were often the subject of local legends or ritual practices. At some wells believed to have curative properties, rags torn from sick persons' clothing were hung on nearby trees (this was believed to help the healing process), and at wishing wells it was customary to throw bent pins or bent coins into the water. Well names with pagan associations occur repeatedly in village records, among which we may note the many tree wells (*Ashwell*, *Nutwell*, *Oakwell*, etc); wells at which offerings were made (*Farthingwell*, *Pennywell*); wells used for divination or magic (*Elwell*, *Fretwell*, *Runwell*); and wells with names drawn from pagan mythology (*Thurswell* = giant or demon well, *Nickerswell* = well haunted by a water-spirit, *Puckwell*, *Hobwell*, *Mabswell*, etc).

2. Hermit Wells. Hermit wells are common in Wales, Ireland and Cornwall, and there is a fine example at Weem in Perthshire. Hermits were much influenced by notions of sacred geography and tended to settle by springs which flowed out of cliffs or rock outcrops (recalling the miracle wrought by Moses in the wilderness), and sometimes at sites which could only be approached by a single narrow path ('for strait is the gate and narrow is the way that leadeth unto life, and few there be that find it – *Matt. 7 :14*). When a hermit well bears the name of an early British saint it is not because the well was subsequently dedicated to his or her memory but because the saint actually lived there and used the well; or because it belonged to a monastery which was founded by the saint. They are thus a very special link with our early Christian past.

3. Church Wells. These wells supplied the church with water for the font and other liturgical purposes and in some cases may have been used for baptisms before any church building existed in the neighbourhood. Commonly they are found in or near churchyards and sometimes bear the same dedication as the church. In many cases however they are known simply as 'the holy well' (though not all 'holy wells' are church wells or even always Christian).

4. Relic Wells. A small number of wells are associated with the bodies of kings and saints which are said to have been washed in a well, or to have rested by it, or (in one or two cases) to have been buried and exhumed, giving rise to a spring (a common folk motif). Sometimes a saint is said to have been beheaded by pagans and to have picked up his head and washed it in a nearby well before piously expiring! There are obvious associations here with the Celtic head cult, and relic wells tend to occur in areas where Celtic influence persisted, eg. the south-west and the Welsh borderlands.

5. Medieval Wayside Wells. During the high Middle Ages, holy wells became part of a richly devotional landscape. Everything, it seemed, was waiting to be invested with Christian meaning. Attention thus turned to wayside wells and wells on the perimeter of villages, and many of these were blessed and dedicated, mostly to St Mary, though also to other major saints like St Anne, St Catherine and St James. To these we may add wells with Christian-sounding names or attributes. Thus wells associated with the *ellern* or elder tree (or even with a mythical 'Ellen' of pre-Christian cult) could now be plausibly reinterpreted as wells anciently dedicated to St Helen. (The cult of St Helen *was* ancient, but a fair number of Helen wells are situated in fields or woodland and are thus likely to be late adoptions). Sometimes one can still find hedges or small groves of holly trees growing beside wayside wells – remnants of a former sacred avenue or enclosure. They are an almost certain sign of a late medieval dedication.

6. Spa Wells. At the Reformation, pilgrimages to holy wells were forbidden, well chapels fell into ruin, and the cult of the saints was abolished. Fortunately for springs and wells the Reformation coincided with the discovery of chemical analysis. Cures at wells which had once been thought miraculous could now be explained as owing to the mineral content of the water, and the next three centuries saw the growth into fashionable elegance of towns like Bath, Buxton, Cheltenham and Harrogate. Some villages with mineral springs (like Stoney Middleton and Llanrhaeadr – gazetteer) failed to attract the well-to-do and settled down instead to cater for a trickle of humbler visitors. In this way, a number of Welsh hermit wells enjoyed a second lease of life and still have their (mainly eighteenth century) immersion baths – generally rectangular, sometimes enclosed by walling, and usually open to the sky.

7. 'Romantick' Wells During the late seventeenth and eighteenth centuries, country houses were rebuilt on a grand scale and landscape gardening came into fashion. Follies, grottoes and Romantick vistas were now all the rage. If a landowner was lucky enough to have a holy well in his newly-created park it was likely to be prettified with a classical façade, a lion's head mask or a Grecian urn. If he wasn't so lucky he might invent one by christening or rechristening an ordinary spring. Many a well-lover has speculated about the Roman origin of this or that well dedicated to Diana without bothering to enquire whether the land once belonged to the local hall. Almost invariably it will be found that it did. Most of the Robin Hood wells probably date from this period or a little earlier, and in some cases may have been re-named by the local peasantry. Deciding which 'romantick' wells have a real history can be a difficult task.

8. Wells with personal or secular names. Under this category we include all the wells which do not fit neatly into any of the other categories. Some of them may be wells which once bore a Christian dedication but which were secularized in the wake of the Reformation. During the seventeenth century the Holy Well or Abbey Well at Whitby began to be referred to as 'the Low Well'; at Gordon in Berwickshire, St Oswald's Well, which is close to the church, is now called 'the Harewell'; and at Hampole in South Yorkshire the former monastery well, which must certainly have been dedicated to a saint, and which had close associations with Richard Rolle, is nowadays known simply as 'Town Well'.

The Reformation had other, unforeseen consequences. When a sacred landscape is despoiled of its shrines and its saints the result is not an unrelieved sterility. Other, less reputable figures tend to move in and take up residence instead: ghosts, witches, murderers, forsaken lovers, village eccentrics and the like. Legends and customs begin to attach to wells which had formerly been Christian, like St John's Well at Mount Grace Priory, which became a popular wishing well, and perhaps to some wells which had never previously enjoyed any sort of cult.. Even today, to a tiny minority of the population, wells tend to evoke an earlier, more mysterious world. *Woodwell* at Silverdale and *Gawton's Well* at Knypersley have both been described as 'very spiritual places'. And since not much seems to be known about them we are entitled to believe that they may be heirs to a rich and forgotten past. Perhaps they are.

(The foregoing classification works well for Britain, but it is becoming increasingly apparent that a 'theology' of holy wells is very ancient indeed and common to all the Indo-European peoples. Fish wells, for instance, are frequently described as Celtic but they occur also in the Middle East and in India. Spectacular examples can still be seen below the Pandav Falls near Khajuraho in Madhya Pradesh and at Mahakutl in Karnatika. Many Hindu temples have associated sacred wells or pools, and springs associated with rock outcrops are a common feature of hermit sites whether Christian, Hindu or Buddhist.)

THE GAZETTEER

For most well-enthusiasts nothing is so frustrating as to undertake a long journey to a well only to find that it no longer exists or that the water has ceased to flow (though in the latter case there may still be things to learn from the topography of the site). A spring or spring-fed well is a living thing, unique and personal, differing from other springs in its mineral composition, in the way it flows, perhaps in taste and colour, and in less tangible ways. A well-basin or well-house, deprived of its water, is a mere shell; of interest perhaps to architects, folklorists and historians, but not a 'thou' in Martin Buber's famous sense, and therefore not something with which one can enter into psychological communion. We touch here on something that lies at the very heart of ancient religion (and to which some Christians – notably those from the Orthodox/Catholic end of the spectrum – can often intuitively respond). At any rate we think it important to stress that the wells and springs discussed in the Gazetteer section were all flowing freely when we visited them. Beyond this our aim has been to select wells which are significant objects visually or have some obvious point of interest. Most of them are to be found in towns or villages or close to a road. In the very few cases where they involve a twenty or thirty minute's walk we have tried to ensure that the walk itself is pleasant and/or that the end result justifies the effort. Finally, and as the title of the book suggests, these are wells which, with one or two exceptions, have not featured significantly in previous national surveys, though nowadays brief references to most of them can be found on the web.

NOTE: Except in the case of the new county/unitary authorities of Lincolnshire and Yorkshire, where the old name is preserved in the new one, we have used the old county names to facilitate cross-referencing with earlier works – eg. the many county and regional surveys.

Former hermit well: Pandav Falls India

GAZETTEER

ALKBOROUGH, NORTH LINCOLNSHIRE

THE KELL WELL

Alkborough is a pretty village with a number of ironstone cottages grouped around a raised, circular churchyard. SW of the church is a medieval turf maze – one of only nine still surviving in the UK – and from here an ancient trackway runs south along the brow of the ironstone scarp to Burton-on-Stather. At Alkborough the scarp reaches its highest point and there are fine views over the Vale of York. Closer at hand is the even more impressive sight of the rivers Trent and Ouse converging to form the Humber.

To reach the Kell Well follow the trackway south for half a mile. The well is just below and to the right of the footpath and there is a flight of steps leading down to it. The water issues from beneath a shallow stone arch and from pipes set higher in the retaining wall, and descends to the River Trent by a series of tiny waterfalls.

Currently (2010) there is a dispute on the Web about the age of the well and its status. We cannot think why. Flint arrowheads and other

Neolithic implements, including a stone axe-head, have been found in or close to the well and we ourselves have picked up fragments of hand-thrown pottery from it. Clearly the well has a very long history, though whether the implements were left there accidentally or as votive offerings, who can say? The well is also known locally for the star stones which still occasionally litter its bed. These are fossil crinoids, or in plain English, the segmented stems of primitive sea-lilies, and they occur in two forms. Sometimes one finds a small portion of the star-shaped stalk; sometimes a scatter of its individual segments. These look exactly like miniature stars and are slightly smaller in diameter than a five-pence piece. They used to be collected by children, who called them "kestles and postles". It is possible to guess that the 'kestles', or castles, were the intact stalk portions, which do bear a vague resemblance to castle keeps; and that the 'postles' were the detached star segments. The Kell Well is also, at times, a petrifying spring, but this quality in its water seems to come and go. 'Kell' is Danish *keld* or *kelda*, meaning a spring, and testifies to the Viking colonization of this corner of Lincolnshire (cf. Burton Stather, from Old Norse *stoth*, a landing-place or jetty).

Fifty yards north of the church, at the side of the byway which runs downhill to Alkborough Flats, are LOW WELLS: easily missed, since the three small arches that encase the springs are only about a foot high. They are set side by side in a brick retaining wall and the water flows into a long rectangular trough. Not much is known about these wells, though they may once have been associated with the church.

Low Wells

BATHAMPTON, SOMERSET

THE DOG'S HEAD SPOUT

Lion's head masks used to be a common feature of public drinking fountains, but at Bathampton a spring issues from a garden wall in the main street through a larger-than-life cast-iron dog's head, filling a stone trough. It is, to say the least, an unusual object, and its charm is enhanced by the strong flow of water from the spring.

The origin of the Dog's Head is a bit of a mystery. No-one seems to know when it was cast, or by whom, or who presented it to the village. The cottages to the east of the spout are named 1 –3 Dog's Head Cottages. They were built in 1906 and replaced two older dwellings that were called Dog's Nose Cottages. One of these is mentioned in the 1881 Census, and the spout must therefore be at least that old.

The spring which feeds the Dog's Head rises higher up the hillside but is now piped directly to the spout. It has never been known to fail and is thought to have been always the main source of water for the village. Phil Quin (*Holy Wells of Bath and Bristol Region*, p.160) repeats a statement of Dom Ethelbert Horne that the trough 'may once have been used as a bath for curative purposes.' Like certain other of Dom Ethelbert's surmises this one should be taken with a grain of salt. There are hundreds of similar troughs up and down the country; it does not in the least resemble an immersion bath; and we know that at one time the spring first filled another trough higher up the hillside. Beyond that, try submerging yourself in it! It is however likely that in Roman times the spring was associated with a nearby villa.

In any case a delightful curiosity.

BODMIN, CORNWALL

ST GURON'S WELL

Perhaps the most impressive town well anywhere in Britain. The spring rises in a now padlocked well-house close to the west front of the parish church but is piped to another well-house on the outside of the churchyard wall. Here it discharges with considerable force through the mouths of two gargoyles, into a stone trough. Above the gargoyles is an inscription bearing the date 1545. A third, even more powerful jet issues from a cavity in the side of the well-house to form a triangular pool of beautifully clear water beside the pavement. The Cornish antiquary Richard Carew (1555-1620) had Protestant prejudices about 'well-worship' and tried to discredit this one, arguing that the water was contaminated by the bodies in the churchyard. Actually, as Thomas Quiller-Couch observed (*Ancient and Holy Wells of Cornwall*, 1894, pp.80-81), the water 'comes through glazed pipes from a great depth, and interments in the churchyard have long been discontinued.' The fact that the water flows so strongly and is unaffected even by prolonged drought shows that it has its origin in a subterranean reservoir, almost certainly at a great distance from the churchyard.

Some people claim that the well was originally dedicated to St Petroc, but this is almost certainly not true. St Guron seems to have settled here in the sixth century, but the cult of St Petroc was transferred from Padstow to Bodmin (perhaps, as Canon Doble suggested, to avoid piratical raids) at some time before the eleventh century. As in many other cases where a change of church dedication took place, the church well would seem to preserve the original dedication – in this case to St Guron, whose personal water supply it almost certainly was.

Two other Bodmin wells are worth visiting:

ST PETROC'S WELL

In Priory Park, beyond the football ground, situated just below a railed enclosure called the Skate Park. It forms an attractive pool below a grassy bank and is overhung by beeches, oaks and holly trees (and perhaps formerly by hazel bushes, to judge from the presence of a young sapling). This was probably the chief water supply of a monastery dedicated to St Petroc in the Middle Ages, of which no other trace now survives. A wooden statue of the Virgin was discovered here in 1908 and is now in Buckfast Abbey.

SCARLETTS WELL

Situated north-west of the town centre, close to the Camel Trail. Park in the Camel Trail car park at Scarletts Well Road and walk westwards. A gap in the hedge, 50 yards from the car park, gives access to a metalled lane which leads directly to the well. A notice beside the well states:

> ## SCARLETTS WELL
>
> OF ALL THE BODMIN HOLY WELLS, SCARLETTS WELL WAS THE MOST RENOWNED. THE WELL POSSIBLY BELONGED TO THE PRIORY OF BODINIEL AND WAS NAMED AFTER THE PROMINENT SCARLETT FAMILY, WHO PROVIDED THREE MPS FOR THE TOWN BETWEEN 1312 AND 1341

Quiller-Couch remarked that the water remained at a constant temperature of 53°F throughout the year and that its weight was similar to distilled water.

Carew in his *Survey of Cornwall*, c.1600, wrote that rumours spread throughout the land concerning the healing properties of the well. So widespread was the report, that people flocked here in huge numbers and the justices of the town, finding the use of the well overwhelming, cordoned off the spring and forbade its use.

Since the people of Bodmin presumably benefited financially from the influx of visitors, the closure of the well can only, one would think, have been ordered for puritanical reasons. It was the sixteenth-century version of political correctness, and every bit as nasty.

Scarletts Well is nowadays a less than reliable spring. It is best visited in winter when the flow can be impressive and the water creates a sizeable pool (there is no well basin). In a dry summer it dwindles to a mere trickle.

CAISTOR, LINCOLNSHIRE

THE SYFER SPRING

At the bottom of Fountain Street. It was described and illustrated by William Stukeley in his *Itinerarium Curiosum* (1724, vol.1 p.102 and vol.2 plate 20). In those days it ran in several streams down a stone cascade and thence into a sunken rectangular pool with stepping stones, although Stukeley remarks that it had been known to pour down the cascade with great force in a single wide sheet. The cascade itself was built of "great stones laid flat like a wall and joined together with lead" and Stukeley judged it to be a genuine Roman survival. Nowadays the spring issues from a niche in a garden retaining wall, filling a handsome quarter-circular pool just beside the pavement. This must have been one of the town's major wells in Roman times and was almost certainly dedicated to a Roman, or local, god or goddess. Yet there is no surviving folklore (a common problem in Lincolnshire) and very few clues to its later history.
A point to note is that although the Syfer Spring is close to the church it seems never to have been associated with it, despite its size and

impressive appearance. By contrast the church spring (the Holy Well), which is less than fifty yards from the Syfer Spring, must always have been a small affair and is now so insignificant that it is concealed beneath a grating at the foot of the Folly Steps. Here as in numerous other cases, a modest, nameless spring seems to have been adopted by the Church in preference to a more obvious one with a known or presumed history of cult. The point would seem to have wide application.

Syfer is an Anglo-Saxon word meaning 'pure'.

CALVERTON, BUCKINGHAMSHIRE

GORRICK'S WELL 9SP788393)

Stony Stratford and Calverton are separated by a very short stretch of open countryside and here is Gorrick's Well, situated just below a lay-by at the side of the road connecting the two villages. It lies approximately 200 yards north of the *Shoulder of Mutton* Inn. There are steps leading down to the well and the water discharges from a lion's head spout into a rectangular stone tank with concrete surrounds.

According to James Rattue (*The Holy Wells of Buckinghamshire*, Umbra Press 2003), 'the name has not been explained, but a story relates that the water was used by a witch's pupil to give a blind gypsy tinker back his sight.' R. Ewart Bailey (*Romance Around Stony Stratford*, 1928), quotes an old rhyme:

> When Gorrick's spring flows fast and clear
> Stoop down and drink, for health is here.
> If Gorrick's Spring should e'er run dry,
> Beware, for Pestilence is nigh.

Readers who have studied our introductory remarks on the classification of wells (pp.10-13) should have no difficulty in deciding to which category this one belongs..

CATTISTOCK, DORSET

CHURCHYARD WELL

It is thought that the village of Cattistock was given to the monks of Milton Abbey in 934 – though the surviving (English) charter is post-Conquest and the Latin copy is spurious. We know however that the monks built a church here in the twelfth century. The question arises: was this the first church on the site or did it replace an earlier one?

English church wells are almost exclusively Anglo-Saxon. For some unexplained reason the Normans, when they built a church on a new site, seem not to have worried about the absence of a nearby water source, although water was of course required for baptisms, ablutions, and the mixed chalice at the Mass. The existence of the well at Cattistock thus raises a strong presumption in favour of an Anglo-Saxon church here, though it is impossible to be sure. The fact that a spring happened to rise in what became a part of the churchyard might just be coincidence. It is however a prime (defensive) site, and an early church would make sense topographically as well as historically.

The well was restored with stone surrounds when the church was rebuilt by Sir George Gilbert Scott in 1857. It is a handsome object if you like gothic ornament, is in a good state of preservation, and the spring still flows freely. It deserves to be better known.

CONISBROUGH, SOUTH YORKSHIRE

THE HOLY WELL

On the north side of the A630, a few yards beyond its junction with Holywell Lane. Park in a side street and walk to the well. Conisbrough is spelt *Cunugesburh* in a document of 1002-4 and *Coningsburg* in Domesday Book: 'the King's Stronghold' – ie. a royal borough. At one time the parish church had seven dependent churches or chapels and is known to have been an early minster. Conisbrough must have been time out of mind a vital defensive site commanding the River Don and the (Roman?) road from Rotherham to Doncaster, and it is worth noting that early minsters sometimes began as British churches before the Anglo-Saxon conquest. In any case we may surmise that Conisbrough was an important site in the British kingdom of Elmet, which survived until 616 (or 626). Recent excavations in the Wellgate area of the town confirm that there was a settlement here in the 2nd-3rd century.

The Holy Well is mentioned in a glebe terrier of 1764 and must therefore be medieval if not earlier. It issues from the base of what was evidently once a massive rock outcrop. Most of the outcrop was quarried in the eighteenth/early nineteenth century but the springs (or some of them) survive and still flow quite freely. The well is away from the settlement nucleus but is unlikely, on account of its name, to have been a medieval wayside well. In fact it looks uncommonly like a sixth century hermit site. We know that British – ie. Celtic – Christianity had established itself in the area since there were British churches at Ecclesfield and Ecclesall. It is thus probable that the ecclesiastical significance of the well derives from an early unknown British saint.

Despite the almost continuous stream of traffic along the A630 this is an attractive and atmospheric spot – perhaps one of the earliest Christian sites in South Yorkshire.

EAST AYTON, NORTH YORKSHIRE

OLD MAN'S MOUTH

This well is 1¾ miles north of the village in scenic Forge Valley, a densely wooded gorge-like ravine cut by meltwater at the end of the last Ice Age. It is easy to find since it lies beside the road, immediately opposite a car park and picnic spot, the entrance posts of which are carved with the name of the well.

Normally a well is an excavated spring. Here however the spring lies about 100 yards higher up the hillside at the top of a precipitous v-shaped valley, and the separation of spring and well was a practical necessity. (Imagine toiling up and down the hillside with heavy buckets and the ever-present risk of losing one's footing).

There seems to be no surviving folklore but Whelan and Taylor include the well in their *Yorkshire Wells and Sacred Springs* on the assumption that the name has pagan associations. It discharges a copious volume of water and, whatever its previous history, is now honoured as a rag-well.

FOUNTAINS ABBEY, NORTH YORKSHIRE

ROBIN HOOD'S WELL

It is at least very appropriate that there should be a Robin Hood's Well at Fountains Abbey since, according to a ballad extant in both the Percy and Child collections, Robin had a notable encounter here with Friar Tuck:

>When Robin came to Fountaines Abbey,
>Wherat that fryer lay,
>He was ware of the fryer where he stood,
>And to him thus can he say:

>'I am a wet weary man,' said Robin Hood,
>'Good fellow, as thou may see;
>Wilt beare me over this wild water
>Ffor sweete Saint Charity?'

The Friar does, grudgingly, carry him across the river but then produces a longsword and demands that Robin carry him back. Robin does so, and then demands to be carried across the river once again. The Friar refuses, Robin blows his horn, and his men appear with bows in their hands. Nothing daunted, the Friar whistles sharply, and fifty huge dogs come running up! There would seem to be a moral here. At any rate peace is restored and Friar Tuck joins Robin in the Greenwood (*The Ballad of the Curtal Friar*).

The Robin Hood ballads go back at least to the fourteenth century. Langland, in his *Piers Ploughman* (c.1377) puts into the mouth of an idle clergyman the words:

> I ken noght parfitly my *Paternoster* as the preest it syngeth,
> But I ken rymes of Robyn Hood ....

A Robin Hood's Well is mentioned at Burghwallis in 1622, and 'the stone of Robert Hode' was recorded in the same parish as early as 1422. There is also a reference to a 'Robin Hood's Bower' at Oughtibridge in 1637. At Fountains Abbey, the earliest topographical reference is to 'Robin Hood Wood' (1734). The name could be earlier but the abbey grounds were then being landscaped and romantic names were much in fashion. The well is still known locally by some people as 'St Mary's Well' – presumably its original dedication. It is situated a few yards from the footpath which hugs the River Skell on its south bank – ie. on the opposite side of the river to the abbey ruins. Unfortunately it is not nowadays a very active spring and often ceases to flow, especially in summer and early autumn.

As its name suggests, Fountains Abbey is a region of springs, some of them still free flowing, though their names or dedications seem not to have survived. One of them feeds a well adorned with fragments from the abbey which is recessed into the boundary wall immediately opposite the West Gate entrance kiosk. A second well, set within a brick arch, is at the back of the courtyard which adjoins Fountains Hall on its west side. This must have been the Hall's original water supply though like the well near the kiosk it was doubtless utilized in the first place by the monks.

Two anonymous wells which contributed to the name Fountains Abbey

FROME, SOMERSET

THE HOLY WELL

The present church of St John the Baptist is medieval, heavily restored in the 19th century. However the first church on this site was founded by St Aldhelm c.685, and it is not therefore surprising to find that there is a church well. This was restored and elaborated c.1860 by the Revd William Bennett, a well-known Tractarian, who also created an impressive *Via Dolorosa*, a processional stairway leading from the well through the graveyard to the north transept, decorated with almost life-size sculptured figures. At the same time the well was provided with a monumental gothic canopy, and this, together with the sculptured frieze, forms an imposing ascent to the church.

The outflow from the well is culverted for a few yards and then emerges in an open conduit, running down the middle of Cheap Street, as it has done since at least the sixteenth century. The antiquary John Leland mentioned the conduit in his well-known *Itinerary* c.1540, though at that time it seems to have extended into other streets. It is still one of the minor delights of the town.

Unfortunately when we visited Frome at the end of May we found that the well had been "decorated" for the feast of St Aldhelm. The main embellishment took the form of a large oblong board, screwed into the masonry of the well to form a display of art-work by some of the local

Sunday school children. Whatever the merits or demerits of the display it could surely have been designed more imaginatively so as not to obliterate the view of the well-basin and its impressive fountain. We gather, however, that the board is only in place for about two weeks in the year .

The *Via Dolorosa*

GIGGLESWICK, NORTH YORKSHIRE

BANK WELL

Turn downhill off the main road and then right at the T-junction into Bankwell Road. You will see the well ahead of you, beside the gated entrance to the Old Vicarage.

The spring flows out of a walled bank into a rectangular stone trough and overflows the trough at the other end, disappearing down a grating. The area around the well forms a tiny paved courtyard where those wishing to draw water must formerly have waited their turn. The site is thus an attractive piece of social history and the spring still flows freely. The water is mildly chalybeate.

What makes the well particularly significant is the fact that a tiny lead figurine was found here during the nineteenth century. It was originally thought to be a Tudor toy since the figure is female and wears what appears to be a sixteenth-century hooped skirt. Subsequently it was identified as a product of the Celtic La Tene culture ($5^{th} - 1^{st}$ century BC). It was originally displayed in the Pigyard Museum in Settle but is now in private hands. A drawing of the figurine can be found on the Web (*Bank Well – Megalithic Portal*).

One assumes that it was placed in the well as a votive offering. An important well therefore and almost certainly a very ancient cult site.

GREAT ASBY, WESTMORLAND (now CUMBRIA)

ST HELEN'S WELL

Visually this is one of the most attractive wells in the north of England though remarkably little seems to be known about it. Various writers have conjectured about its history and origins (eg. Taylor Page, *Cumbrian Holy Wells*) but nothing can be said about it with certainty except that the name is at least medieval and just possibly earlier. It is first mentioned in a survey of 1777. How old is the village? Again, no-one knows. The name is Norse (*Aschaby*, c.1160: a settlement[1] where ash trees grow), but it could have had an earlier name. The village is situated at the junction of two streams, and an ancient bridge ('the bridge of Patrick') is mentioned in a will of 1374. Patrick dedications tend to be pre-Conquest and imported from Ireland by Christianized Norse settlers who had previously lived there. If the bridge itself is pre-Conquest it would suggest a significant early settlement. The parish church is dedicated to St Peter (first reference 1229).

A point to note is that the well is fed by a very powerful spring, and 'great' springs seem nearly always to have been venerated by early man. It could be that the present name of the well points back to an earlier, non-Christian name like *Ellern Well* (Elder-tree Well), though since it is close to the church it is also possible that it preserves the name of an earlier church dedicated to St Helen.[2] Whatever the truth of the matter the well is likely to have had a long history. However see also the next entry.

The well is situated on a riverside green, beside the (augmented) village beck, into which it discharges with considerable force. It is a large rectangular stone structure, approximately 14 feet by 11½ feet, and currently about 12 inches deep. (Was it once much deeper? If so, why?) It would be an eye-catching object anywhere but is much enhanced by its greensward/riverside setting.

---

1. The tendency to assume that Scandinavian *–by* meant a farm is generally wrong. Usually it seems to have meant 'village', but 'settlement' would perhaps be more accurate. Some places with the *–by* suffix can be shown to have been fairly significant places when the Danes renamed them, eg. *Derby, Rugby, Whitby,* etc. Clearly too the many places called *Kirkby* or *Kirby* could not have been mere farms.

2. As noted in the next entry (Great Hatfield), early church dedications to St Helen were uncommon, and more likely to have been British than Anglo-Saxon. Cumbria was, however, a very Celtic area (the name derives from *Cymru,* the Welsh), and British Christianity lingered longer in these parts. An early church or monastery dedicated to St Helen is thus quite possible.

GREAT HATFIELD, EAST YORKSHIRE

ST HELEN'S WELL

200 yards SE of the village, next to the old graveyard, by the side of the road to Withernwick. There was a chapel here in 1492 which was also dedicated to St Helen. It was almost certainly one of the many chapels-of-ease which were founded in the fifteenth century for the convenience of people who lived a long way from the nearest church. In fact despite its name, Great Hatfield has only ever been a hamlet.

According to the Revd William Smith writing in 1923, the water at that time flowed out of a grassy bank. However the well was restored and re-dedicated in 1995, and a good deal of Victorian brickwork was discovered in the process. At the same time the well was provided with a low wall and the present handsome canopy. An inscription on the wall of the well informs visitors that this is a rag-well and claims that it was dedicated to St Helen by the first Christian settlers (an odd idea, for when the English settled here they were *not* Christians, add to which the dedication is almost certainly medieval). The inscription concludes with a verse, also by the Revd William, associating the cult of St Helen with rag-well customs.

Smith was the author of a very readable little book, *Ancient Springs and Streams of the East Riding of Yorkshire*, A. Brown and Sons 1923, which is now something of a collectors' item (our own copy cost us £25 fifteen years ago). He was a keen collector of folk-lore, a man who loved the countryside and observed things closely, and most of his conclusions have stood the test of time. However the claim which he advances in his book, that Helen wells are generally rag-wells, does not stand up to close scrutiny. Rag-wells clearly pre-date the dedication of wells to St Helen and are essentially pagan.

Contrary to popular belief the cult of St Helen in Britain is mainly medieval. It is often argued that St Helena, being Roman, must have been widely venerated by the early British Church, but if so, one would expect to find surviving evidence of this in Wales and Cornwall. In fact Welsh and Cornish dedications to St Helen are very thin on the ground and it is uncertain whether those that do exist refer to the world-famous St Helena, mother of Constantine the Great, or to a British princess called Elen Luyddog, who became the wife of the Roman Emperor Magnus Maximus. In England, the Anglo-Saxon Church showed little interest in St Helena, favourite dedications being those to St Peter, St Paul, St Mary, and other New Testament figures. Indeed, to the best of our belief only two English dedication to St Helen can be confidently dated before the Norman Conquest – ie. the church of St Helen at Abingdon (Berks), and the church and associated well at Kirkby Overblow (North Yorks). There is also the very ancient church of St Helen at Worcester (dedication before 969 and probably pre-Saxon). What seems to have caused the sudden explosion of dedications to St Helen in the Middle Ages was Geoffrey of Monmouth's fictional history, doubtless because he claimed, erroneously and outrageously, that she was the daughter of King Cole or Coel of Colchester, and therefore British by birth.

Now the medieval cult of St Helen coincided with the great age of the Christian well cult, and in particular with the Christianization of many wayside wells and field springs, some of which came to be dedicated to St Helen. This explains why most Helen wells are to be found by the roadside or in fields or woodland – ie. away from the settlement nucleus. Among these wells there must have been some 'ellen' wells, which owed their name to the *ellern* or elder tree, or even to a goddess 'Ellen' of pre-Christian cult, which could now be plausibly interpreted as wells anciently dedicated to St Helen. Some of these wells were probably rag-wells and, despite clerical disapproval, are likely to have continued as such, leading to a synthesis of Christian and pagan customs.

Or the association of rags with Helen wells may have occurred at a later date. Following the Reformation, Christian holy wells were disowned by Protestant churchmen and ceased to feature, liturgically or ceremonially, among the Church's concerns. Pre-Christian customs began to attach themselves to wells which had previously been venerated for their Christian associations, and here again the rag-well custom had an opportunity to transfer itself and invade new territory. (The world-famous 'Cloutie' Well at Munlochy in Scotland is an obvious case in point. Here the original dedication was to St Boniface). No doubt the Revd William observed the association of rag-well customs with Helen wells in his own area of East Yorkshire (where there are several Helen dedications) and assumed that the link was specific. He was wrong, but it was a pardonable mistake.

Before 1995 this well was virtually unknown outside the pages of Smith's book. It is still one of our lesser–known wells, but a current website suggests that it must now be one of the ten best wells in Yorkshire! Readers may be grateful to those living locally who had the vision to restore it so tastefully. It shows what can be done, even today.

GREAT MALVERN, WORCESTERSHIRE

THE MALVHINA SPOUT

Malvern spring water is, of course, internationally famous, and it can be sampled and collected for free at about twenty locations within the town. Among the most notable of these is Belle View Island, at the junction of Church Street and Worcester Road. There are two public drinking fountains here, both designed by local sculptor Rose Garrard: the Enigma Fountain, commemorating the composer Edward Elgar, which was unveiled by HRH the Duke of York in 2000; and the Malvhina Spout, named after a legendary Celtic princess, which was unveiled in 1998. Both fountains deliver water from nearby springs, and this is twice filtered before emerging here for public use. They are eye-catching, attractive sculptures, but whereas the Enigma Fountain emphasises the aesthetic appeal of water, the Malvhina Spout hints at something darker and more mysterious in our earlier relationship with it.

HACKNESS, NORTH YORKSHIRE

BRIDGE SPRINGS

A nunnery was founded here by St Hilda of Whitby in 680. The parish church still contains Saxon work; and the fragments of a Saxon cross, with an inscription to a certain abbess Æthelburga, are preserved in the north aisle.

A few hundred yards east of the church three springs (one of them called Hilda Spring) unite to form a tiny stream which, in its augmented form, must once have formed the monastery's water supply. Nowadays it is culverted for a short distance and then emerges (to baffle credibility) from beneath the pier of a stone footbridge! Thereafter the stream is canalized and flows within a stone conduit or runnel at the side of the road, strongly reminiscent of the runnels which carry water along Trumpington Street in Cambridge. After passing the church the stream joins Lowdales Beck, and their joint volume feeds an artificial lake, created by enlarging the old monastic fishponds. These 'improvements' were part of an ambitious landscaping project carried out between 1795 and 1825 by Sir Richard Vanden Bempde Johnstone, and the canalized stream was perhaps designed as a reminder of his student days at Cambridge University.

In addition to these curiosities Hackness is worth visiting for its parkland elegance and historical associations. Of the three contributory springs, two lie on private land close to the bridge but the third (the largest) follows the road from its source ½ mile east. It rises above a rock pavement worn to the shape of a shallow tiled roof.

HOLYWELL, HUNTINGDONSHIRE

THE HOLY WELL

There was a church here before the Norman Conquest, and since the well is in the churchyard we might conclude that this is just another Anglo-Saxon church well. But things don't add up. The village was already called *Haliewelle* at the time of the Domesday survey, and English (as opposed to Welsh) churchyard wells only came to be regarded as holy during the Middle Ages. In Anglo-Saxon times, a well might bear the name of a saint but it did so, ostensibly at least, merely as a mark of ownership – ie. to denote that the well belonged to a church or monastery founded by (or in the name of) the saint in question. There is something odd here, therefore, and very few clues as to what it might be.

We can surely dismiss the idea that this was a pagan *haelwelle* (omen well) which was taken over by the Church. Anglo-Saxon churchmen were highly sensitive to the charge of 'well worship' and tended to leave pagan wells severely alone. However this is fen country, where British (ie. Welsh) communities seem to have survived undisturbed, in some cases well into the seventh century, and some of them may have been Christian, and served by British priests.

One wonders too if there is any indirect connection with the discovery at nearby St Ives c.1001-2 of a stone sarcophagus. This was found to contain the remains of a bishop, recognizable as such by the inclusion in the coffin of a chalice and certain Episcopal ornaments, and was improbably claimed to be that of Persian bishop named St Ivo. If however the body was that of a *British* bishop who had ministered locally, that would almost certainly explain the origin of the church and well at nearby Holywell. However this is mere speculation. All we can say at present is that here was a well belonging to an Anglo-Saxon church which was venerated long before it ought to have been. A curious well therefore, and one which deserves further research.

HOPE BAGOT, SHROPSHIRE

THE HOLY WELL

Despite the fact that its tiny basin contains only a few inches of water this is a well not to be missed.

The early history of Hope Bagot is obscure. The oldest portions of the church are twelfth century, and the village is not mentioned in Domesday Book. It is possible that it had been a casualty of the war between Gruffudd ap Llywelyn, king of Wales, and the English, and was at that time depopulated. Whether there had been a church here before then is anybody's guess.

The well is just inside the churchyard, near the foot of a steep bank which descends to a sunken lane. What is interesting is that the spring rises between the roots of a truly enormous yew tree which was evidently planted there as guardian of the spring and to increase the virtue of the water. The associations of the well are thus at least partly pagan. The tree has a spectacular girth (c.24 feet) and is almost awesome in its grandeur, especially when viewed from the lane. Unfortunately it cannot be dated since the trunk is hollow and the heartwood is missing. One can guess however that it is at least as old as the present church and possibly older. At the time of our visit (summer 2010) its lower branches were festooned with polyester ribbons, a lady's handkerchief, and a necklace! Obviously some visitors believe that it was once a rag-well.

The well-nigh universal belief that Christian holy wells had pagan origins is mostly wishful thinking. The Anglo-Saxon Church for instance was consistently hostile to any form of well worship. However Hope Bagot is in an area that remained for centuries culturally Welsh, and the Welsh were happy to perpetuate the occasional pagan custom. We see it in the association of Welsh hermits with pagan fish wells. Whether the Hope Bagot yew tree is any more significant than that – ie. whether it marks an ancient cult site – seems to us doubtful, though of course one cannot be sure. In any case an important well, and one that deserves to be better known.

KINGSTEIGNTON, DEVON

THE HONEY WELL

At the eastern end of Kingsteignton churchyard is a wrought-iron gate which gives access to a narrow, walled footpath. Follow the path southwards and downhill. A short distance from the gate is a walled enclosure on the left-hand side in which the spring rises. It is not a very significant well but it is reputed to have healing properties, and if you happen to be in Kingsteignton it is worth a short detour.

A local inhabitant who directed us to the well remarked: 'Nobody knows where the water comes from.' Now in a small way this is a petrifying well, and the action of the water on the vegetable growth below the mouth of the spring produces small quantities of honey-coloured tufa. The water must therefore percolate through Jurassic limestone beds – presumably those on Golver's Hill at nearby Rydon, which were quarried last century to provide stone for Buckfast Abbey.

Perhaps it was the honey-coloured tufa that gave rise to the name of the well?

LINBY, NOTTINGHAMSHIRE

TWO CROSSES, A SPRING AND A WELL

Linby has two crosses and an associated well. The upper cross, at the western end of the village green, covers an ancient spring, now culverted for a few yards to emerge as a steeply banked stream at the side of the B6011. It is then culverted again briefly to emerge from a well chamber beneath the second (lower) cross at the eastern end of the green. The upper cross dates back to the Middle Ages. It was vandalized during the Commonwealth period but restored in 1869. The lower cross bears the date 1663 and appears to have been set up to replace the upper one after it partial destruction – perhaps as one of the many which were erected in mute testimony to the Restoration of the monarchy in 1660.

The upper cross is mentioned in the Forest Perambulation of 1538 and marks one of the ancient boundaries of Sherwood Forest. The original marker at this point would almost certainly have been the spring, and that would explain why the cross was erected directly above it. The well beneath the lower cross may have been intended to symbolize the Living Water which flows, spiritually, from the Cross of Christ (John 4 : 10-14).

See *Linby and Papplewick Notebook* by L.I. Butler (1953), accessible on the web at www.nottshistory.org.uk/butler1953/linby5.htm, from which some of the above information is taken.

LITTLE WALSINGHAM, NORFOLK

SHRINE WELL

> As you came from the holy land
> Of Walsingham,
> Met you not with my true love
> By the way as you came?
>
> *old ballad*

In 1061 in Walsingham, a devout and wealthy woman had a vision of the Virgin Mary and was told to build a shrine in her honour. The central feature of the shrine was to be a 'Holy House', in imitation of the house in which Mary was living when she was visited by the Archangel Gabriel. In 1169 an abbey of Augustinian Canons was founded to care for the shrine, and during the Middle Ages Walsingham became one of the most famous places of pilgrimage anywhere in Europe.

At the Reformation the abbey was suppressed and the shrine destroyed – perhaps no place in Britain was so hated by the new breed of Protestants – but memories lingered. In 1931 the Anglican Vicar of Walsingham refounded the shrine; pilgrims and tourists came in growing numbers, and it was twice found necessary to extend the building. It now comprises a labyrinth of tiny chapels, a small church, and, right at the heart of the building, as a climax to the pilgrims' peregrinations, an imaginative reconstruction of the Holy House itself. The exterior of the shrine is modest and spare-looking but once inside the visitor is transported into a world of splendour and mystery quite at odds with the secularizing tendencies of contemporary Western Christianity. Here, as perhaps nowhere else in Britain, it is possible, by simply immersing oneself in the atmosphere of the building, to recapture something of the mystical spirit of the Middle Ages.

During the rebuilding of the shrine a well was discovered – thought by many to be the original holy well of the medieval shrine, and its water is always freely available for the use of pilgrims and visitors.

There are also two former healing wells (rectangular tanks with stone surrounds) in the grounds of the abbey, just east of the ruins of the former abbey church. They still contain water but have a rather neglected and stagnant appearance and are nowadays regarded as mere wishing wells.

One of the wells in the grounds of the abbey.

LLANRHAEADR, DENBIGHSHIRE

FFYNNON DDYFNOG

St Dyfnog is an obscure figure from the Age of the Celtic Saints (c.450-650) and is said to have lived here as a hermit. Local tradition has it that the spring owes its healing properties to the fact that he did penance here by immersing himself in the icy-cold waters while saying his prayers. Dyfnog has sometimes been identified (or confused?) with St Domnoc (Mo-Domnoc to the Irish), the disciple and beekeeper of St David, who later settled in Ireland and is said to have introduced beekeeping there. St Dyfnog and St Domnoc are both commemorated on 13th February, which is suggestive, and Leland referred to the spring as 'Fonnon Dunnoc; St Dunokes Welle a mighty spring.' As to its virtues, Edward Lhuyd, in his *Itinerary* (1699) says that it was 'a Bath much frequented; the water heals scabs and itch, etc. Some say 'twould cure ye pox.'

Like certain other Welsh wells its popularity was sustained by the spa cult – Welsh curative springs were the poor man's version of Bath or

Harrogate. The site possessed changing rooms and a large immersion bath, and Thomas Pennant, the Welsh travel writer, who visited Llanrhaeadr c.1780, says that 'the fountain was inclosed in an angular wall, decorated with small human figures and before the well for the use of the pious bathers.' It sounds like a pre-Reformation survival. However the buildings have long since disappeared, and all that remains is the oblong immersion bath.

The water still issues with great force from the back of a small cwm. It was originally thought to be a remarkably copious spring but is now known to be the product of two streams that rise in the neighbouring parish of Prion. These disappear down limestone sink-holes and flow underground for two miles, during which they unite, before emerging here at Llanrhyaeadr. The well water is thus 'twice born' and might be accounted more potent and mysterious on that account.

Llanrhaeadr is 3 miles SE of Denbigh, just off the A525. Access to the well is via a gate in the south side of the churchyard wall. From here a woodland path hugs the stream uphill to its source.

LLANTWIT MAJOR, GLAMORGAN

SPRING (ST ILTUD'S WELL?)

Llantwit Major is an important place in Christian history for it was here, apparently on the site of the present parish church, and towards the end of the fifth century, that St Iltud established his famous monastery. We owe most of what we know about him to a nearly contemporary biography of St Samson, who founded the cathedral city of Dol in Brittany and was one of Iltud's pupils. Iltud's monastery was also a school, and Iltud himself 'the most famous master of the Britons... accomplished in all the scriptures, in philosophy, geometry, rhetoric, grammar and arithmetic.' The British monk Gildas, writing about 540, is almost certainly referring to St Iltud when he speaks of a local king having had as his teacher 'the most refined master of almost all Britain.' Gildas himself, St Samson, St Paul Aurelian, and (according to some sources) St David, are all said to have been educated at Iltud's monastic school. They were probably pupils there at about the same time.

Just outside the churchyard, beside the lane which skirts it on its western side, is a small stream which has its source in a spring situated to the north of the village. However this stream is also fed by another spring close to the churchyard gate, which emerges from the laneside bank and is at first channelled separately behind a long kerbstone. It is a tiny affair nowadays but was almost certainly the original monastery spring from which water was drawn by Iltud and his illustrious pupils. During the Middle Ages it probably bore a dedication to St Iltud. Pilgrims may be glad to know of its existence.

MALHAM, NORTH YORKSHIRE

MALHAM COVE

Malham Cove is, of course, world famous, and readers can be forgiven for wondering why it features in a survey of lesser-known wells and springs. Or is it simply one of the more curious?

Curious it certainly is, but also breath-taking. No river in Britain has a more dramatic birth than Malham Beck. It steals out, already a sizeable river, from underneath the Cove's 240 feet sheer cliff; and although purists will insist that this is *not* the true source of the River Aire, it is certainly one of its sources, and until fairly recently was assumed to be the only one.

Well-lovers tend to be a conservative race. Apart from the occasional 'discovery' of a well previously unrecorded, most writers go on using Victorian information and thinking in Victorian terms. A cult well is a well around which folklore and legends have gathered, and folklore is almost always assumed to be ancient, although in some cases it is not. The discovery of an ancient artefact in, or close to, a well is also (and rightly) seen as evidence of its antiquity and cult status. But what if a well, spring or river source has lost its ancient folklore, as must often have happened? There is still a marked reluctance to apply historical or topographical principles to the study of springs and wells, although these things can add greatly to our knowledge of certain sites. The neglect of Malham Cove is an obvious case in point.

Rivers feature prominently in many religions. The Ganges, the Yamuna, the Narmada and the Godavari are still the sacred rivers of India, visited annually by countless thousands of pilgrims, and many rivers are known to have been sacred to the Celts. The River Seine (Celtic *Sicauna*) means 'sacred river', the Scottish Don was *Devonia*, 'Goddess', the Dee (old Welsh *Deva*, the Roman name for Chester) was 'the Goddess' or 'the Holy One'. The etymology of the River Aire is uncertain but may derive from old Welsh *Isara* meaning 'Strong One', which the Celts would be very apt to personify.

The source of a sacred river was considered especially holy and mysterious. In India, three very important pilgrimages are to Yamunotri, source of the Yamuna, Gangotri, traditional source of the Ganges, and Amarkantak, where the subterranean Narmada 'reveals herself at last to the anchorites of Shiva, deep in meditation around the holy tank' – ie. the holy well of Amarkantak (Gita Mehta, *A River Sutra*, p.4). There was a Celtic temple at the source of the Seine, and from its site nearly two hundred wooden figure carvings have been retrieved (Bord, *Sacred Waters*, pp.5-6).

All this has obvious implications for Malham and the River Aire. But Malham has one further thing to offer - the great cliff from which Malham Beck so visually and perpetually receives its birth. Sacred springs were almost routinely associated with gorges, cliffs and caves. Again there are examples from India, and at Delphi in Greece, once famous for its Oracle, a sacred spring rises from the base of a not dissimilar cliff. The Ancient Greeks called it 'the Glad Mountain' because they found it terrifying in its grandeur and were anxious to placate the local god or goddess by giving the place a friendly and cheerful name! May we not infer something of the same ancient dread in respect of Malham Cove? That the locality was sacred to the Celts (and perhaps to those who lived there before them) is suggested by the fact that at nearby Gordale Scar, precarious yew trees still grow on some of the inaccessible ledges. No other yew trees grow naturally anywhere in or around Malham (there is no churchyard), and the simplest explanation is that they are the third or fourth generation descendents of a once sacred avenue or grove.

Never mind the fact that this is what is technically known as a resurgence. Malham Cove deserves a place in any survey of springs and wells partly because it is a significant water source, and also on account of its sheer magnificence. But the cult argument deserves to be taken very seriously.

Where the beck emerges from the Cove

MATLOCK BATH, DERBYSHIRE

PETRIFYING WELL

For thousands of years the thermal waters of Matlock Bath have deposited tufa on the hillside to a great depth. At several places where the waters now surface there are 'tufa' wells – ie. small mounds of mainly calcium carbonate over which the water flows on a self-created embankment usually terminating in a cascade. Some of them, like the one next to the tiny jetty immediately below the Grand Pavilion, are in deeply shaded places and are now bare of vegetation and roughly the colour of mud. However two of these wells are spectacularly festooned with mosses, trailing grasses and other moisture-loving plants. Gradually this vegetation gets coated with calcium and petrifies, and the well 'grows' accordingly in height. The one which is illustrated is at the southern end of the Riverside Gardens (Lovers' Walk) but there is another one in Temple Road beside the fishpond. They are extraordinary objects and well worth viewing.

MIDDLESMOOR, NORTH YORKSHIRE

THE BLACKSMITH'S WELL

At the upper end of Nidderdale. The village sits on top of the fell, reminding one curiously of hilltop settlements in France and Spain. It is austerely picturesque. Everything here is built of stone, and away from the main road the houses cluster between grass-grown cobbled alleyways. It could be a nineteenth century film set. Twenty yards west of the pub is a fine spring now called the Blacksmith's Well, and there is a small well in the churchyard. First as to the church.

The present building is Victorian but there were at least two earlier churches on the same site. Inside are a Norman font and the upper parts of an 11th century Anglo-Saxon hammer-head cross bearing the inscription 'Cross of St Ceadda' (ie. Chad), to whom the church is dedicated.

One would not expect a dedication to Chad in such a remote spot. Middlesmoor is in the diocese of Ripon, and a dedication to St Wilfrid would be less surprising. Early dedications to Anglo-Saxon saints are anyway uncommon and generally denote some direct association with the saint in question. However Chad was, briefly, bishop of York (665-7) and it is possible that the dedication commemorates an early monastic cell founded here under his direction. An elevated location would make sense, and down below, by a scoured tributary of the Nidd, is How Stean Gorge, a likely hermit site. The cross too is of a type often set up to mark a former monastery or early Christian foundation.

What is interesting from our point of view is that the church was built not on the brow of the hill but somewhat lower down. Doubtless its exact location was determined by the church spring; but this is now a very feeble affair, often ceasing to flow entirely during the summer months, and is unlikely ever to have been as vigorous as the Blacksmith's Well. Why was not the church situated above the latter – ie. higher up the hill, which would have given it a commanding position? There could be more than one reason, but the likely explanation is that the Blacksmith's Well had pagan associations and was thus shunned by the church. That, of course, increases its interest for well-lovers. It rises by the side of the main road and flows out of a grassy bank into a pair of stone troughs. Despite its workaday appearance it is an eye-catching feature, and the water still flows freely. The name 'Blacksmith's Well' is recent, and connects the well with the former smithy, now converted to a private dwelling, situated in a cobbled recess just to the right. For much of the twentieth century the well water was used to temper iron and steel implements, and for part of that time it doubled as a horse trough. Before piped water came to the village it was used for domestic purposes and was the chief spring of the village. Its original name seems to have been lost.

The church spring: now often quite dry.

NEWTONDALE, NORTH YORKSHIRE

NEWTONDALE SPRING (SE841953)

Take the steam train from Pickering and alight at Newtondale Halt (request stop – see the guard before boarding the train). This is by far the most convenient way to view the spring as there is no road to Newtondale, but it does involve a careful consideration of the railway timetable which varies a good deal throughout the year. (During the winter months there are weeks on end when no trains run.) After leaving the railway station you come to a T-junction of woodland paths. Turn right here – ie. north-east – and after about half a mile, look for a green Forestry Commission sign pointing left and uphill (*Newtondale Spring and Picnic Spot*). From here the route is well signposted but the route is fairly strenuous and involves a scramble over tumbled rocks. Allow one hour for the round walk, and longer if you wish to linger by the spring.

Early man lived thickly hereabouts and his burial places or tumuli are found everywhere on the moors. There are over 3000 of them taking the North Yorkshire Moors as a whole, and well over a hundred within a three mile radius of the spring. There are also stone circles, cairns, Iron-Age dikes and 'celtic' fields. Although we have no direct evidence that the spring was a cult site in prehistoric times, its later history, vivid colour and petrifying qualities suggest that it was. The reddish staining shows it to be richly chalybeate and the water tastes strongly of iron. It has the curious property of making the spring seem 'bloody' and transparently pure at the same time. Like almost all chalybeate springs it was once highly regarded for its health-giving properties.

In the eighteenth century and no doubt much earlier, a Midsummer's Day fair was held here to which people came at least partly 'to perform certain ceremonies which ensured them the blessing of the well.' * In fact Midsummer festivals were held all over Europe. They came to be known as St John's Day festivals. Bonfires were kindled on the hilltops and rituals were performed to purify the local waters. Whatever the precise nature of the Newtondale 'ceremonies' they were almost certainly an outgrowth of customs like these.

In the seventeenth century two cisterns and a well-house were built around the spring for the benefit of bathers and its waters were recommended 'for restoring limbs and joints'. However by 1817 the site was ruinous, and before the arrival of the railway in 1836 the fair itself had been discontinued. The surviving stone steps were probably associated with one of the seventeenth century baths.

The spring is now provided with a viewing platform and an information board to which we are indebted for some of the foregoing details.

---

* J. Murray, *Handbook for Travellers to Yorkshire*, London 1874.

NORTH CAVE, EAST YORKSHIRE

ST HELEN'S WELL

The entrance to this well is about 200 yards west of the church on the north side of the main street. Approaching from the church you first pass a public footpath (also worth exploring) and then a stone cottage called Quaker Cottage (No.14). We recommend that you call here and ask for permission to view the well, but if there is no answer, simply proceed. We understand that access is never refused.

At the left – ie. west – side of the cottage is a private strip of grass ending at a small gate. Go through this, and through another gate, and you find yourself in a very spacious park-like garden with a fine sward and mature oak trees. It is a place where one can meditate or simply rest and soak up the atmosphere. The well is just beyond the second gate, close to the right-hand side of the path. The outflow is culverted for a few yards and then emerges as a tiny rivulet flowing north towards the village beck. Doubtless on account of its delightful setting this is some people's favourite well.

Many Yorkshire wells are dedicated to St Helen, probably because she was the mother of Constantine the Great, who was proclaimed emperor of the Roman world by the legions at York. As mentioned earlier she came to be thought of as a British princess. In fact she was born in Bithynia, the daughter of an innkeeper, and seems never to have set foot in Britain. She is famous for her visit to Jerusalem in 335, where she was involved in the discovery of the true Cross.

The well was, for a time, better known as the Quaker Well because a Quaker meeting house once occupied the site of the present cottage. The base of the well is circular, with stone coursing, presumably the remains of a medieval well-house. The dedication too is almost certainly medieval.

SAWLEY, NORTH YORKSHIRE

WINE WIFE WELL

Three miles west of Fountains Abbey as the crow flies (grid reference 232674).

A minor road from Sawley leads west to a junction with the B6285. Just before the junction, on the left hand (west) side of the minor road is a lay-by. Park here and consult the information board which can be reached through a gate on the opposite side of the road. This gives directions to the well.

Alternatively, walk back along the minor road for fifty yards and bear right down the farm track which leads into the woods. Twenty yards down this track, again on the right hand or west side, is a rustic arch and a wooden walkway leading to the well.

The spring rises in a tiny box-like cavern, set among heather and bracken and surrounded by oak and alder trees. The name of the well has caused some head-scratching, but '*Old* Wife' was a term long used for the mother goddess of ancient paganism (cf. *Old Wives Well* on the North Yorkshire Moors). *Wine* is (or can be) an Anglo-Saxon word meaning 'friend' or 'protector'. Put the two together and we have what is probably a variant name for the same goddess. In any case a name which suggests the well's considerable antiquity.

People who visit this well expecting something elaborate will be disappointed. But for those who like peace and quiet, heathland and nature unadorned, it is a small gem.

SILVERDALE, LANCASHIRE

WOODWELL

Woodwell is extraordinarily difficult to photograph, at any rate when the leaves are on the trees. If you try for a panoramic view, all it shows are (1) the large rectangular overflow pool with its railed surrounds, and (2) a line of trees screening what looks like a steep scarp slope in the background. In fact Woodwell is a gem: even today a fairly active dropping well with a shallow, cave-like arch, set into the base of a formidable cliff face.

The later history of the well was very workaday. Writing in 1906, Henry Taylor summed it up as follows:

> The water from this well flowed into a drinking trough, the surplus flowing into troughs for washing clothes, and then two enclosures for cattle. The drinking water trough and one of the cattle enclosures survive – *The Ancient Crosses and Wells of Lancashire, volume 1: Lonsdale Hundred*, revised and re-issued 1999.

What of its early history? If we assume that the low-lying ground in front of the well was once more marshy than it is now (a very reasonable assumption, given that the existing overflow pool acts as a reservoir, and that water extraction has almost certainly reduced the flow from the well), then Woodwell had all the classic ingredients of an early Celtic hermit site: the spring, the cliff face, the tiny island of space where the hermit had his cabin, and the narrow approach path. It would be strange if, in this most Celtic area of England, early hermits had not discovered such an ideal location and exploited it..

To reach the well, drive or walk westwards through the village along Stankelt Road, and when the houses begin to peter out, turn left (southwards) on to Lindeth Road. About 300 yards down the latter, on the left-hand side, is a metalled track leading into the woods (signposted Woodwell Lane). This goes directly to the well, and there is a patch of hard standing where you can park and turn the car. Even today it is a remote and atmospheric spot.

Woodwell: approach to the well.

SOUTHAM, WARWICKSHIRE

THE HOLY WELL

A semicircular pool with stone surrounds and three heavily weathered stone heads through which the water discharges into a second, sunken chamber with steps at each side. This is one of the best preserved and visually attractive wells anywhere in England and is a grade 2 listed structure. The water still flows very freely.

The listed building text conjectures that the well structure is "probably seventeenth-eighteenth century with possible earlier origins." Given the known history of the well this is perhaps over-cautious. The well lay on glebe land in the Open Fields but in 1701 the Rector was exempted from any expense concerning its maintenance. This suggests that repairs were expensive and that the well was already an elaborate affair – a supposition strengthened by the Enclosure Award of 1761, which refers to the stonework and again exempts the proprietors from maintaining it.

The stone heads have been assessed as "perhaps medieval", and since the well was never part of a private estate it is difficult to see who would have gone to the expense of providing them in the post-Reformation era. They are surely more likely to have been part of a design commissioned by Coventry Priory, to whom the manor and advowson of Southam belonged in the fifteenth century. The fact that the well was known throughout the Middle Ages as 'the holy well' is also suggestive. It is, as one might expect, a mineral spring, and the quality of the water is said to have been a factor in the establishment of a private eye and ear hospital in Southam in 1823. In about 1918 a latten brass calvary was found near the well and is now in the south aisle of St James' parish church.

To reach the well, walk or drive along Park Lane, which leads west from the north side of the parish church, and turn left into Wattons Lane. At the foot of the hill, fork left into the cul-de-sac, which is the continuation of Wattons Lane – look for the street sign. From here, a footpath (sometimes muddy) leads directly to the well. It is advisable to wear wellingtons.

The well was restored in 2005-7 with the help of a Heritage Lottery Grant.

STEVINGTON, BEDFORDSHIRE

THE HOLY WELL (SP990536)

Down a footpath which skirts the east end of the churchyard. The spring issues from beneath a brick arch on the outside of the churchyard wall. A second, lesser spring trickles from beneath the wall only a few yards away. The ground around the well is a conservation area noted for butterbur (a plant with leaves rather like rhubarb).

There was a church here before the Conquest (the lower third of the tower is believed to date from the early 10th century) and the Holy Well looks like a typical Anglo-Saxon church well. In fact it seems to have been – or to have become – more than that since there was a hospital here in the Middle Ages, 'described in 1812 as a range of low stone buildings, with traces of a gatehouse or porter's lodge, and an unroofed chapel' (A.J. Fleming, 'The Church of St Mary the Virgin, Stevington, *Archaeological Journal No.139*, 1982, pp.54-55).Presumably it catered for sick pilgrims who came to Stevington to drink or bathe in the well water. Perhaps the well was responsible for a miraculous cure or was associated with a vision of the Virgin, and thus acquired a more than local reputation?

Fleming suggests that the site may have been the focus of a Celtic water cult, for which there is evidence at other places along the Ouse valley. However paganism would have had to have been, at best, a dim memory for the Anglo-Saxon Church to build here – see Appendix B.

STOKE ST MILBOROUGH, SHROPSHIRE

ST MILBURGA'S WELL

Park in the cul-de-sac which leads to the church and walk back to the T-junction. Turn left here and follow the lane uphill - a matter of 150 yards or so. Almost at the top of the hill you will see a small gate with a cast-iron standpipe beside it giving access to a patch of woodland. The well is 20 yards inside the wood and there is a paved footpath with a handrail.

The well basin is a small rectangular affair with a back wall of dressed stone inscribed 'ST MILBURG'S WELL'. There is water in the well but virtually no flow since the spring is nowadays culverted to by-pass the well, emerging from beneath the footpath at the opposite side. Here it discharges vigorously from a pipe set between two rocks before tumbling down a miniature ravine. Wear wellingtons if you wish to view or photograph the spring from below, for the banks of the stream are muddy and slippery, there is no footpath, and the only way down is by the bed of the stream. If you wish to drink the water do so here and not at the well basin. It has an excellent taste.

From c.703 the land hereabouts belonged to St Milburga's Priory at Much Wenlock, which is presumably how the well got its name (and, via the church, also the village). *Stoke* commonly signified a monastic cell. The well is rich in folklore though most of the legends are variants of those found at other wells (the pursued maiden, the indelible bloodstain – in this case the result of a near-fatal fall from a horse -, the miraculous spring welling up to commemorate the event). There are other elements too including the miraculous ripening of a field of corn. It is all there in Hope for those who want to read it (*The Legendary Lore of the Holy Wells of England*, pp.140-141). The well was first recorded in 1321.

After the Reformation it became a common clothes-washing place though the legends persisted. It also had (or acquired) a reputation for curing sore eyes – another common folk motif. The well "was covered over and altered c.1873 and altered again in 1906. By 1945 its water was piped to six houses" – *VCH Shropshire*, vol.10, p.383.

STONEY MIDDLETON, DERBYSHIRE

THERMAL SPRING (ST MARTIN'S WELL)

This is one of several warm springs (temperature 64°F, 17.7°C) which formerly flowed through the village – the others have been culverted. It used to be thought that Stoney Middleton was a classic case of site continuity: an originally pagan well which was converted to Christian use in the Anglo-Saxon period if not before. This now looks extremely unlikely. The fact is that we know very little about the history of the well before the eighteenth century. The Romans probably utilized it, for its outflow passes close to the foundations of a Roman villa, and they may have venerated the spring, though there is no surviving evidence that they did so. However the Anglo-Saxons seem to have paid no attention to it, at any rate from a Christian point of view, since there was apparently no church here before c.1420, and even then it was merely a chapelry to the church at Hathersage. Thereafter the well was dedicated, like the church, to St Martin, though whether it was ever a focus for pilgrims is not known. In the eighteenth century a bath house existed, though again there is no firm evidence as to its age, and the waters were extolled by a Dr Short in his treatise *Mineral Waters* (1734). He described the bath house as being 'enclosed with a wall four yards high, four square, six yards every way. On its inside is a stone walk, and it is open above.' It sounds very much like a primitive spa complex. In 1815 it was replaced by the present Roman style bath house in Blind Lane (currently undergoing restoration).

The spring forms an attractive small channel just east of the bath house and some of its water fills a stone trough at the side of the road. It has a 'flat', rather unsatisfying taste. The well is dressed – though apparently not every year – on the last Saturday in July.

TOTNES, DEVON

THE LEECHWELL

A weirdly impressive and atmospheric well which deserves to be better known. It is now used as a place of worship by the town's New Age community and is usually decorated with flowers and ribbons (to signify its presumed status as a rag-well).

Three springs rise here, each with its rectangular stone trough. At least from the Middle Ages the springs were visited for healing purposes, and the three troughs acquired the names *Toad*, *Long Crippler* (a local word for the harmless slow worm), and *Snake* ! It has been conjectured that *Toad* cured skin diseases, *Long Crippler* eye complaints, and that *Snake* was used in the treatment of snakebite and psychological disorders. The Leechwell was included in a list of sites patrolled by two town wardens in 1444.

Leechcraft was the art of healing, and 17th-18th century doctors were sometimes known as *leechers*. Hence presumably *Leechwell*: a medicinal or curative well.
To reach the Leechwell, take the narrow passage which leads downhill from the side of the Kingsbridge Inn

TROUTBECK, WESTMORLAND (now CUMBRIA)

VILLAGE WELLS

Troutbeck does not seem to attract well-lovers. Arguably its saints' wells have no real history, being ordinary village wells which were named in the latter part of the 19th century, and its other wells have no folklore and lack even the squalid untidiness which sometimes betoken a genuine or spurious rag-well. The fact is that Troutbeck is altogether too picturesque, spruce and well-cared-for!

And yet Troutbeck is one of a mere handful of places which preserve their ancient system of village wells. Not only that but each well is a minor architectural delight. Say, if you like, that they are all 19th century prettifications and that they conform to two standard types: the well-trough, recessed into a bank at the side of the road (the "saints" wells); and the drinking-fountain type, with its familiar edifice and embrasure. Nevertheless taken as a group they are an irreplaceable piece of social history, and they add a good deal of discreet charm to what is anyway a very attractive village. They deserve to be visited, appreciated, and better-known.

References on the Web are mainly to the three well-troughs, each of which has its name inscribed in gothic lettering on a large stone slab set into the back wall. Their attractiveness is enhanced by the dry-stone walling of their surrounds, the moisture-loving plants that grow out of their crannies, and the fact that they all still flow. There is St John's Well and St James' Well – but what is the name of the third one? Web users have taken to calling it St Margaret's Well, but the inscription is purely secular: 'Margaret's Well'. In fact all three structures were erected by a local landowning family, the Dawsons, who also owned *The Cragg* and (latterly) *Birkhead*, both of which are near the sites of the wells. They are reputed to have been named after members of the family (certainly James and John were both family names) and why the label 'Saint' was attached to two of them is not known. Perhaps the gentlemen, being of a modest disposition, preferred to hide their identities behind those of their saintly namesakes!

The roadside bank where the three wells occur also gives rise to two quite powerful springs. They issue from box-like cavities and flow down dry-stone channels before disappearing under the road.

One of the drinking fountains

Wayside spring

UPWEY, DORSET

THE WISHING WELL

In the main street, just beside the lane which leads to the church, is an attractive café called *The Wishing Well*. Ask here to view the well (no charge is made but donations are encouraged). The well is at the top of the garden behind the café, and access is through the shop.

The Wishing Well is a curious blend of the sublime and the silly. Here is a great spring, issuing from cracks and joints in a rock floor to form a majestic stream 25 feet wide in places. It is in fact the source of the River Wey, as the name of the village suggests (Upwey – 'the upper Wey' or '[place] up the River Wey'.

The well was first recorded in 1212 as Elwell (from Old English *haelwelle*, an omen spring) and was clearly pagan in its associations. The current parish church guide tries to link the church with the well but this is pure wishful thinking. The well is at least 200 yards from the churchyard and seems never to have been called 'the holy well' or to have borne a Christian dedication. Nor is it the nearest or most accessible water source. Another thing that would have condemned the spring in the eyes of superstitious churchmen is its gravity-defying quality. Like an eighteenth century canal, the stream hugs the contour of the hillside instead of falling rapidly to the valley floor. In fact what we have here is a pretty clear case of the medieval church *refusing* to adopt a pagan well (cf. Caistor).

With the advent of the spa cult the spring began to attract attention as a healing well, although it is not in the technical sense a mineral spring. George III was in the habit of visiting the well and drinking the water, and a gold cup was kept at a nearby house for his exclusive use. According to local tradition it later became a race trophy and the origin of the Ascot Gold Cup.

The arrival of the railway brought a fresh influx of visitors and a *Wishing Well Halt* was provided at nearby Broadwey. The arched seating area behind the well was built in 1887 to commemorate Queen Victoria's Golden Jubilee. Meanwhile, pseudo-antiquarianism and Victorian commerce intervened to make it look more like the popular notion of a wishing well. This led to the construction of a circular stone parapet over the most active of the springs and the excavation of a shallow well shaft, into which coins could be dropped for good luck. A sunken stone trough would have been much more in keeping but I suppose we should be thankful that the 'improvements' didn't extend to a canopy and a bucket! It is all quite phoney and unnecessary, and, to those who know anything about water sources, a painful excrescence which merely spoils the natural grandeur of the site. According to James Rattue the well was also provided with some spurious folklore 'borrowed from St Augustine's Well at Cerne Abbas and which, in any case, appears to have derived from a novel' (Rattue, *The Living Stream*, p.134).

The garden in which the spring is situated is, however, an unqualified delight. Some of the water from the stream is admitted through sluices and channels to create a most attractive water garden, and summer visitors can enjoy tea and cakes on an outdoor terrace amidst a profusion of lilies and other water-loving plants.

Despite the Victorian commercialism and the well that isn't a well, this is a site which is eminently worth visiting. Few springs are as impressive or as picturesque as this one.

WATNALL, NOTTINGHAMSHIRE

THE HOLY WELL

Travel SW along the B600 towards the centre of Watnall, passing a pub called *The Queen's Head*. Turn right into Trough Road, and then right again into Trough Lane. The well is on the right hand side.

Visually it is not anything to write home about. The flow of water is at best sluggish, and the one surviving item of folklore may be no older than the nineteenth century. But this is a well worth viewing for historical reasons. In the first place the spring has altered its course, for it used to rise a few yards further north. Note the miniature cliff face – its original back wall. Secondly though, and of particular interest, are the remnants of a former holly hedge behind and to the north of its former site. Almost certainly this once formed part of a sacred avenue through which pilgrims passed as they approached the well, and it defines the site as a medieval holy well of some importance. There are vestiges of a similar avenue at St Helen's Well, Kirkby Overblow (North Yorks).

The existing well bears a bronze plaque with the following inscription:

> Holy Well
> According to folklore in the nineteenth century, a small boy who lived opposite was not expected to live. Here a priest baptized him and he recovered. Thereafter the well was considered holy.

It is extremely unlikely that this story dates from the Middle Ages though it may refer to a real event. In any case the well would seem to have been venerated at least as early as the fifteenth century.

WELLS, SOMERSET

ST ANDREW'S WELL AND OTHERS

Great springs were perhaps always cult sites in prehistoric times, and the springs at Wells are certainly great. Those that rise in the garden of the Bishop's Palace discharge approximately 4 million gallons a day (40 gallons per second). We know that Stone Age man lived hereabouts and that there was some sort of Romano-British settlement here, though present evidence suggests that it was a very small one.

The Cathedral occupies the site of a Romano-British mausoleum, which was contained within a larger square building. Rodwell (1981) thinks that it may have been a shrine to a Christian martyr. This building was replaced by a mortuary chapel, presumably when the Saxon minster was founded by St Aldhelm, c.705.

James Rattue summarizes the problem thus:

> It is quite obvious that the wells were the focal point of the minster settlement; the first record of the place name is Fontanelium in 725 and in 766 we hear of 'the minster which is situated next to the great spring which is called wielen….' Yet there was then no kind of Christianization

– no 'halliwelle', no 'Seyntandreweswella' – and nor is there any indication that at this time the well was seen as anything more than a notable spring. (*The Living Stream*, 1995, p.58).

Clearly the dedication of the spring (or springs) to St Andrew came later. Most of these problems disappear if we assume that the mausoleum was indeed raised over a Christian martyr. The place would then have become, like Verulamium, a pilgrimage site, and may have developed into a British (ie. Welsh) monastery. Why else would the Anglo-Saxon Church have raised a mortuary chapel over the mausoleum; and why else (unless a religious foundation already existed there) would such an otherwise apparently insignificant settlement have been selected as the site for an Anglo-Saxon minster? It may be objected that, in that case, we should expect the name of the saint to have been perpetuated in the place-name – as Verulamium became St Albans.

Yet this is not an insuperable difficulty. At Lincoln too, the early church of St Paul-in-the-Bail seems to have contained the remains of a Christian martyr, though his (her?) name is unknown. Even St Albans is in this respect a very dubious example. Was the martyr really called Alban, or had his real name been forgotten, so that his first hagiographer called him simply Albanus, meaning 'a Briton'? The Romano-British Church does not seem to have been particularly good at remembering the names of its saints.*

The fact that the springs were not at first venerated is in accordance with what we know about the early English Church. Water was, of course, required for liturgical purposes but great springs, together with petrifying wells, drumming wells, blood-red chalybeate springs, ebbing and flowing wells and the like, were innately suspicious, as tending to pagan 'well worship'; and unless such a site was already Christian (eg. monastic, or a shrine) it is not likely to have been regarded as a suitable place for a church or minster.

At least three of the original wells were subsequently excavated to form the present lake at the north-west corner of the Palace Gardens. On a fine day – ie. when its surface isn't disturbed or pitted with rain-drops – water can be seen surging upwards from the silt; though it is only by watching the tremendous volume of water that pours over the weir into the Palace moat that one can gain an adequate idea of the size and power of the wells.

On the western side of the lake, in an area designated for quiet contemplation but not yet open to the public, are two more pools, one of which is the holy well of St Andrew. Two further springs rise just south of the lake to form similar small pools.

A final delight for the visitor is to view the water which flows in runnels down both sides of the High Street, beginning near the Market Place. These channels too are spring-fed, and where they commence, water can be seen bubbling up from beneath the pavement. They are almost identical in appearance to the runnels which carry water along both sides of Trumpington Street in Cambridge.

---

*So far as we know, the last great persecution (that of Diocletian, c.305) did not affect Britain. Early British martyrs are thus likely to have suffered in the earlier persecutions of Septimus Severus (c.209) or Decius (c.254) when British Christian communities were still tiny and perhaps in many cases less than permanent. In these circumstances it is hardly surprising that names tended to be forgotten with the passage of time, leaving only the dim memory of a martyr's grave.

Water from the wells pouring over the weir.

WHITCHURCH, BUCKINGHAMSHIRE

WHITTLE HOLE (SP801207)

There is a Holy Well at Whitchurch but it is now little more than a muddy pool in a spinney east of the village. By contrast Whittle Hole is perhaps the most visually attractive well in Buckinghamshire. A copious spring of very clear water emerges from a culvert behind a tiny cottage and fills a stone cistern, the back wall of which is adorned with trailing plants, before disappearing down a chute beneath the footpath. The water has an interesting taste, resembling weak tea. According to Joseph Holloway (*Two Lectures on the History of Whitchurch*, 1889) it was 'not held so sacred as the Holy Well' but its water was 'blessed and given to and for the free and good use of the inhabitants.' Before the introduction of piped water this was evidently the village's principal water supply. It is said to discharge approximately 32 gallons per minute in normal conditions and up to three times that amount after heavy rain. 'Whittle' seems to be a corruption of 'White Well'. There is no surviving folklore but the well is nowadays blessed on the Sunday following Ascension Day.

To reach the well, walk northwards up the village street until one is nearly parallel with the lane that leads to the church. Next to a garage repair yard on the left-hand (west) side of the street is a long-established footpath. This leads directly to the well.

WIDECOMBE-IN-THE-MOOR, DEVON

THE SAXON WELL

Three roads meet in the centre of the village close to *The Old Inn*. Take the one which is signposted *Buckland, Dartmeet, Postbridge* and which dips sharply downhill. The well is 50 yards from the inn, near the bottom of the hill, just beyond *Manor Cottage* at the right-hand side of the road. There are two springs, one of which rises in the tiny well-house, filling a stone basin which is much deeper than it looks; and another one which issues from beneath two overhanging stones and joins the outflow from the well in front of the well-house door.

The well-house – and it *is* tiny – a mere 4 feet in height – is built of ashlar granite and dates from the 16th or 17th century. However the name of the well hints at a much longer history, perhaps going back another eight or nine hundred years.

The chief piece of folk-lore connected with the well derives from a real event. It is said that the people of Widecombe gave the devil a drink from the well when he rode into the village on 21 October 1638, and that it sizzled as it went down his throat! On that day the church was struck by lightning and severely damaged, and several people were killed or injured. Another version of the story is that the devil drank not the well water but a flagon of beer at a nearby public house. However the well is reputed to be curative, especially in treating sore eyes (a very common belief in respect of holy wells, perhaps because water can act as a mirror and is therefore thought to resemble the human eye?)

Widecombe is of course much visited because of the old song *Widecombe Fair* ('old Uncle Tom Cobley and all'). The Fair is still held every year on the second Tuesday in September, and the drive from Ashburton is one of the best ways of getting a first view of the landscape and beauty of Dartmoor. Sadly most visitors never notice the well, although some people consider it to be the prettiest in Devon.

WOLSINGHAM, Co DURHAM

THE HOLY WELL

There are two ways to reach the well. (1) Take the B6296, which goes uphill and north from the Market Place, and cross the bridge over the beck. Continue uphill for about 300 yards and then take the lane on the left (Holywell Lane). This leads directly past the well. OR (2) having crossed the bridge, take the second *alley* on the left (in the middle of a long row of houses). This leads to a footpath which crosses two fields and ends at a stile on Holywell Lane. The well is about 50 yards east of the stile. The advantage of the footpath is that it passes a second well: CHAPEL WALLS WELL, which is believed to be a resurgence from the Holy Well. It lies on the right hand side of the footpath at the end of the first field and rises in a small enclosure set into the boundary wall. It is easy to miss this well since it is virtually hidden behind a large holly bush.

To return to the HOLY WELL. Nowadays it is visited on account of its presumed association with two hermit saints: Ælric of Wolsingham (died c.1107) and Godric of Finchale 1065-1170) who lived with Ælric during the last two years of the latter's life. The names of both hermits are commemorated on the wrought-iron gates of the well house. Little is known about Ælric but Godric became famous even during his lifetime. Successively a pedlar, a merchant, a sea-captain and a pirate, he became for the last fifty years of his life a hermit at Finchale near Durham, dying at the advanced age of 105. He had an extraordinary rapport with animals, including snakes, seems to have been gifted with second sight, and is credited with many miraculous cures. His *Life*, by Reginald of Durham, who knew him well and cared for him in his last years, helped to disseminate his cult, though even before Reginald's book appeared (c.1180) his grave at Finchale had become a focus for pilgrims.

Whether the well owes its name to Ælric and Godric is a moot point. It could have been called the Holy Well because the spring rises on land once owned by Durham Cathedral. However Ælric was a former monk of Durham and may have been given permission to settle here. Taken in conjunction with the curious nature of the well house, the probability is that this is where the two saints lived.

The Holy Well is first referred to in a deed of 1724. The listed building text describes the well house as 18th century but structurally it is a bit of a puzzle. It is very large, with a stone-vaulted roof and stone benches along the side walls. The well itself is situated centrally against the back wall but tends to overflow, sometimes quite powerfully, for about half the year. It is doubtless for this reason that the floor of the well house slopes down from the side walls to form a very shallow V, thus allowing the excess water to form a shallow stream which flows under the gates of the well house and empties into a sink just outside the entrance. The water is said to be mildly chalybeate.

In fact it looks as if what we have here is not just an overgrown well house but a genuine well *chapel*, albeit one of unusual design.* It may have been modified when the well structure was rebuilt in the 18th century, though it is possible that it is an Irish-style well chapel, since it closely resembles the one surviving Irish example at St Mullins in County Carlow. This is not as unlikely as it may sound, for Northumbria was evangelized by Irish missionaries in the 7th century. Add to this that almost everything we know about St Godric suggests that he was consciously imitating the early Celtic hermit saints. Could it be that he and Ælric were merely the last of a long line of north-country hermits who endeavoured to keep alive the traditions of their Celtic predecessors? A reasonable inference to be drawn from the well structure is that it marks the dwelling place of a seventh century hermit saint whose memory was perpetuated by the creation of a well chapel, and that Ælric chose to live here for that reason. The fact that the well lies so close to the River Wear is also suggestive. Well chapels were closely associated with river and inshore fishing, and services were held in them to bless the water and thus ensure a plentiful fishing harvest.

---

*British (ie. Welsh and Cornish) well chapels were based on the vision of the New Jerusalem in the Book of Ezekiel, chapter 47, an idealized version of the temple at Jerusalem and the temple spring. British well chapels all had proper channels to conduct the water through the building, and in those cases where the channel emerged by the entrance door it was usually set assymetrically against the right-hand door jamb. But in the (ruined) well chapel at St Mullins the water flows freely through the building, as here.

The other well (Chapel Walls Well).

WORMHILL, DERBYSHIRE

THE BRINDLEY MEMORIAL WELL

On the edge of the village green, sheltered from the road by ornamental trees and shrubs, is a large and impressive Victorian well-house fronted by three interconnected stone troughs. The whole thing has a dignified and formal appearance and is, in fact, a monument to James Brindley the canal engineer, who was born in the nearby hamlet of Tunstead in 1716. The well-house was erected in 1875 and a nearby plaque commemorates his principal achievements.

The spring which feeds the well must always have been Wormhill's principal water supply and it is possible that during the Middle Ages it bore a Christian dedication – perhaps (like the church) to St Margaret of Antioch. However if there was ever any serious well cult it is likely to have been at Wormhill Springs, near Chee Tor, ½ mile south, where well-dressing took place at least as far back as the middle of the nineteenth century.

Nowadays it is the Brindley Memorial Well that is dressed – on the last Saturday in August (the Saturday before the late Summer Bank Holiday).

YEOVIL, SOMERSET

NINESPRINGS

"Why are so many water sources called 'Seven Springs' or 'Nine Springs'?" asks a correspondent on the Web. 'Seven Springs' is certainly a common name, and no doubt reflects an atavistic tendency to settle for 'seven' when there are sometimes six or eight. It is though strange that multiple springs do, quite often, occur in groups of seven!

Beyond this, seven is a sacred number, eg, the seven sacraments, the seven stars, seven days of creation, seven pillars of wisdom, seven ages of man, etc. Coptic theology even has seven archangels. According to the psychologist Carl Jung, the unconscious mind tends to represent totality by the number 4, although most theological systems involve a Trinity, or three senior gods – the fourth part of reality being as yet unredeemed. Add 4 to 3 and we have the sacred number seven. But nine (3 + 3 + 3) is also a feature of some systems:

> Lars Porsena of Clusiam,
> By the nine gods he swore

There are nine muses, nine sacred trees of the druids, nine (sometimes three) roots of the tree Ygdrasil, and Durham Cathedral has a Chapel of Nine Altars. Nine is a number much favoured in magic ritual:

> Thrice to mine and thrice to thine,
> And thrice again to make up nine.

However nine can also be a sinister number, as in Tolkien (the Nine Black Riders). Especially in Norse mythology the number nine is often associated with death. King On sacrificed nine sons; and after slaying the Midgard Serpent Thor took nine steps before he too expired. Slain warriors were carried to Valhalla by the nine Valkyries, etc. As regards springs, seven and nine raise at least a certain presumption in favour of cultic observance. The subject is a fascinating one and invites further study.

The nine springs of this particular entry give their name to a large country park on the southern edge of Yeovil. (Find Wilkinsons in the High Street and walk through the store to the rear entrance. The footpath which leads to the park is across the main road and then downhill, about 100 yards further south.) The area was developed in the nineteenth century as an ornamental park for the Aldon Estate but is now owned and administered by the local council. The springs all rise on the south side of the park in densely-wooded, steep-sided valleys, forming streams which tumble downhill, giving rise to occasional waterfalls, before feeding a large lake which is the park's central feature.

This is an idyllic spot for a country walk: repeatedly uphill and downhill if you want to explore all the paths (stout footwear is recommended and there are places where it can be muddy) – an imaginative blend of the wild and the ornamental in the nineteenth century romantic manner. To those who object that this is an artificial landscape it is perhaps sufficient to reply that, in a certain sense, the English countryside is everywhere 'artificial', for there is hardly a place where it has not been changed and improved in some way. The acid test is whether nature retains the upper hand, and here, for the most part it does –sometimes emphatically so.

The springs themselves are all, in their different ways, minor delights and surprises; in fact three or four of them are as picturesque as you will find anywhere. This was an area which remained demographically Celtic for centuries after the Anglo-Saxon conquest and, especially in view of the name (Ninesprings), it would be surprising if, at some period in their long history, the springs had *not* been the focus of some sort of cult.

Ninesprings : another of the springs

APPENDIX A

THE FOURTEEN BEST WELLS IN BRITAIN – A PERSONAL CHOICE

Lists tend to be controversial and well-lists particularly so since people are attracted to springs and wells for a variety of (often conflicting) reasons. However if everyone named their favourite wells we think that the following would all find a place:

1. **BATH, SOMERSET.** *The Roman Baths Museum.* One of the oldest cult sites in Britain and among the most impressive. Incorporates the famous Hot Spring, the Roman Bath, the King's Bath and many archaeological discoveries. An excellent introduction to the study of springs and wells.

2. **HOLYWELL, FLINTSHIRE.** *St Winefride's Well.* The healing well *par excellence* and the only British water shrine to escape the ravages of the Reformation. An architectural jewel.

3. **BURGHEAD, MORAY.** *The Pictish Well.* A large, circular, semi-subterranean stone chamber into which very little light penetrates. Few wells anywhere in Europe are as strange or puzzling as this one.

4. **GIGGLESWICK, NORTH YORKS.** *The Ebbing and Flowing Well.* Most people find this well disappointing since when they visit it there is nothing to see. But to watch and hear the well when it is in full flow is an eerie and unforgettable experience – possibly Britain's most extraordinary natural phenomenon.

5. **MUNLOCHY, ROSS & CROMARTY.** *The Cloutie Well.* Britain's most famous rag-well, adorned with many thousands of clouts.

6. **BODMIN, CORNWALL.** *St Guron's Well.* A visual delight. See page 20.

7. **PENMON, ANGLESEY.** *St Seiriol's Well.* The archetypal hermit site, remote and atmospheric.

8. **BISLEY, GLOUCESTERSHIRE**. *Seven Wells*. Really one well with seven spouts. Monumental and rich in symbolism.

9. **SOUTHAM, WARWICKSHIRE**. *The Holy Well*. See page 64.

10. **UPWEY, DORSET**. *The Wishing Well*. See page 72.

11. **TISSINGTON, DERBYSHIRE**. *Five Wells*. The mother-place of Derbyshire well-dressing. See especially Hall Well, a tiny gem of classical elegance. The wells are dressed for Ascension Day.

12. **GLASTONBURY, SOMERSET**. *The Chalice Well*. A blood-red chalybeate spring, attractively channelled in park-like surroundings.

13. **TOTNES, DEVON**. *The Leechwell*. See page 69.

14. **ILKLEY, NORTH YORKSHIRE**. *White Wells*. A leftover from the age of the spa cult. Worth visiting for its exquisite keyhole-shaped immersion pool.

Holywell: entrance to the well

Ilkley White Wells

APPENDIX B

CHRISTIANITY AND PAGAN WELLS

Anybody who studies the history of explanations will know that once a bad idea finds its way into print it can soon become conventional wisdom and then come to be regarded as irrefutable fact. People simply assume that because everybody seems to accept it and because it is quoted in all the books the idea must have been shown to be true – quoted from *How To Read a Village*, Richard Muir, Ebury Press 2007, p.39.

The belief that Christian wells – and more particularly church wells - were pagan wells to start with is nowadays an almost universal SUPERSTITION. It is repeated on innumerable websites and in a huge number of parish church guide books, and invites the retort (to quote a character in one of Pinero's plays): 'Doctor, find the bacillus and destroy it!'

As with almost every rule or principle one is going to come across the occasional curious exception; but taken as a generalization it is emphatically and demonstrably untrue. To the early Church the gulf between Christianity and paganism was absolute. It is expressed in the ancient liturgical command: 'Let all catechumens depart!' – ie. before the commencement of the Christian sacrifice. No Church body, whether Roman, British, Irish or Anglo-Saxon, would normally take possession of a functioning pagan site precisely because it would have implied some sort of religious relativism. (In Mediterranean countries, *abandoned* classical temples were sometimes exorcized and re-used, but in Britain and Ireland pagan worship seems to have been almost entirely an open-air affair.) It is true that some (mainly Welsh and Irish) bishops would, in certain circumstances, relax the rule to the extent of allowing, say, a pre-Christian burial ground to be incorporated within a Christian churchyard, but this seems to have been done to reassure first generation Christians that a change of faith would not sunder them from their ancestors (the thinking being that by bringing the dead within consecrated territory they were, in effect, Christianizing them). Celtic churchmen seem also to have been tolerant towards certain minor pagan customs, eg. the intrusion of sacred fish into hermit wells.

In England, however, the (Roman) Church remained for centuries intensely sensitive to the pagan implications of water cults, and 'well worship' was repeatedly condemned by synods and councils. The following is by no means a complete list of pronouncements on the subject but it indicates the strength of feeling which existed throughout the Anglo-Saxon period:

1. 'If in any diocese, any infidel either lights torches or worships trees, fountains or stones, and the bishop neglects to abolish this usage, he is guilty of sacrilege' (*Canon of the Council of Arles, AD 452*).

2. The Penitential attributed to Egbert, Archbishop of York 732-766, forbids the making of offerings to, or vows at, trees and wells (ii,22). Egbert evidently had in mind customs like the offering of coins and bent pins and the hanging of rags on nearby trees. (You don't stop ingrained customs by 'Christianizing' a well, and all the evidence suggests that in the Anglo-Saxon period churchmen left such wells severely alone. After about 1200 attitudes relaxed but, in theory at least, the veneration of any well had to be sanctioned by the local bishop.)

3. 'Every priest … shall zealously teach the Christian faith and entirely extinguish every heathen practice; and forbid worship of wells, and necromancy, and auguries and incantations, and worship of trees and stones…' (the so-called *Canons of Edgar*, 1005 x 1008, quoted in D. Whitelock, M. Brett and C.N.L. Brooke, *Councils and Synods with Other Documents Relating to the English Church, vol.1 AD 871-1204*, Oxford 1981, p.320).

4. 'It is a heathen practice if one worships idols, namely if one worships heathen gods and the sun or the moon, fire or flood, wells or stones or any kind of forest trees' (*Law of King Cnut*, c.1020, quoted Whitelock *et al*, 1981, p.489).

5. 'If there is on anyone's land a sanctuary round a stone or tree or well or any such nonsense, he who made it … is to pay *lahslit* [ie. a fine for breach of the law], half to Christ, half to the lord of the manor' (*The Laws of the Northumbrian Priests*, c.1020-23, quoted Whitelock et al, 1981, p.463).

Other evidence is cited in the Gazetteer – see the entries relating to Caistor, Great Hatfield, Hope Bagot, Middlesmoor, Stoney Middleton, Upwey and Wells. It may not be the kind of thing that most well-lovers wish to hear, but we think it needs to be said.

Well of St Antony the Great, Red Sea Desert, Egypt

If you have enjoyed this book you may also enjoy:

Early Hermit Sites and Well Chapels

by

Ian Thompson

Hermit sites and well chapels are intimately associated with the landscape: with rock outcrops, springs, rivers and other natural features. They came into being at a time when symbolism was still a normal mode of expression and when the distinction between religion and magic was less clear-cut than it is today. This study is an attempt to unravel some of the secrets of these sites and, in the case of well chapels, to show that they are much more unusual and sophisticated buildings than has been generally supposed.

ISBN 978-0-9537067-7-8

With many photographs and diagrams   Price £5.00

Available from leading booksellers or post free
from the publishers at

Bluestone Books   259 Ashby Road   Scunthorpe
DN16 2AB